PALACES AND CHURCHES
OF THE KREMLIN

2

PALACES

AND CHURCHES

OF THE

KREMLIN

EDITED AND INTRODUCED BY PROFESSOR N. N. VORONIN

PHOTOGRAPHS BY KAREL NEUBERT

PAUL HAMLYN LTD · LONDON

ARTIA · PRAGUE

PROGRESS PUBLISHERS · MOSCOW

NOTES ON THE PLATES BY N.Y. MNEVA, M.A., AND V.N. IVANOV

GRAPHIC DESIGN BY JAROSLAV ŠVÁB

DESIGNED AND PRODUCED BY ARTIA FOR PAUL HAMLYN LTD

DRURY HOUSE • RUSSELL STREET • LONDON WC 2

© 1965 BY ARTIA, PRAGUE, AND PROGRESS PUBLISHERS, MOSCOW

PRINTED IN CZECHOSLOVAKIA BY POLYGRAFIA

S 1479

CONTENTS

INTRODUCTION

BY PROFESSOR N. N. VORONIN

To write in brief about Moscow's Kremlin is a formidable task. The Kremlin is more than an imposing architectural ensemble of rare individuality and beauty or a treasure-store of Russian and world art. It is the core and pivot of the history of the Russian people, of the history of Russia's old and new culture whose roots run deep into the centuries. Here art is not to be divorced from history, for without a knowledge of history there can be no appreciation of art. We must therefore look back and let the chronicles and archaeology show us the milestones of history that have largely made the Kremlin what it is today.

In the 11th–12th centuries, a small citadel, the fortified seat of the local boyar Kuchka, stood on the crown of a hill at the mouth of the Neglinnaya, on the site of the present Armoury. Its favourable location at the junction of water-ways and overland routes drew the attention of Prince Yuri Dolgoruky, the masterful ruler of Rostov and Suzdal. He seized the place, and there played host to his ally, Prince Svyatoslav of Chernigov, in the year 1147. He ordered his son, Prince Andrei of Vladimir, to build a small fortress, which was completed in 1156: merchants and artisans flocked to it as to a place of refuge, and by the close of the 12th century a line of powerful ramparts was built around the settlement, which had spread into the plain. This was the town of Moscow, occupying only a third of the area of the present-day Kremlin. In 1238, it doggedly resisted the Mongol hordes.

In the 13th century, as the country recovered from the devastation wrought by the Tatar-Mongols, Moscow gained in prominence; it first became the capital of an unobtrusive principality, which gradually grew stronger and early in the 14th century began a struggle for supremacy in Rus, for the unification of the other principalities under the Moscow princes. The Metropolitan, spiritual lord of "all Rus", moved his seat to Moscow, immensely enhancing the prestige of its dynasty thereby.

The Kremlin, bulwark of Moscow's rise to greatness, underwent a period of radical reconstruction. Its area was considerably increased. Under Prince Ivan Kalita, Moscow builders took a surprisingly short time (1339–1340) to erect new solid oak walls round the fortress—a perimeter of more than 1,600 metres—and dig a deep moat facing the plain to the east.

While remaining a fortress, the Kremlin became a stately residence of the Moscow prince and of the Metropolitan. One by one, four white-stone cathedrals were built on the southern part of Kremlin Hill, which rose high above the waters of the Moskva and towered over the fortress walls. Pride of place went to the Metropolitan's Cathedral of the Assumption (1326); the court Church of Our Saviour (1330) was built near the prince's palace; closer to the edge of the hill rose the royal cathedral-tomb (1333), dedicated to the Archangel Michael, the patron saint of the princes; and in the square, between the latter two, towered the belfry (1329), dedicated to St. Ivan, the author of a book on graduated penance. All these stood on the site of the present-day buildings and formed a well-planned, picturesque ensemble that embodied in stone Moscow's mission of unifying Rus. Its composition and layout determined the subsequent architectural history of the Kremlin. In 1344–1346 all the cathedrals were decorated with frescoes and icons. Greek painters worked on the Metropolitan's Cathedral, and Russians on the others. A chronicler has proudly listed the names of the Russian painters who laid the foundation for the Moscow school of art. *The Chastening Eye of the Lord*, the exquisite *Trinity* and other magnificent icons in the Kremlin cathedrals are some of the glories of the art of that period.

The Moscow principality grew and united to itself Russian lands despite fierce resistance from the princes of Tver and Ryazan, the aggressions of the Lithuanian feudal lords, and the tense preparations for a decisive battle against the Golden Horde. Ivan Kalita's oaken Kremlin, which had burned time and again, no longer suited Moscow's new military and political enterprises. A vast Kremlin, built of white stone, rose swiftly under Grand Prince Dmitry Donskoi, a building feat that amazed the whole of Russia. The giant fortress with nine towers and a perimeter of nearly two kilometres was completed in two years (1366–1367). Its walls ran roughly along the same line as those of the present-day Kremlin. The new monumental pile of the Metropolitan's Chudov (Miracles) Monastery, built near the Kremlin's eastern wall, augmented its architectural ensemble. To commemorate the victory over Mamai's hordes at the Battle of Kulikovo, Princess Yevdokia, Dmitry Donskoi's widow, erected in her half of the palace the splendid Cathedral of the Nativity of Our Lady, with its huge columns. It was built in the style of the famous 12th-century court church of Andrei

Bogolyubsky, autocratic ruler of Vladimir. On the edge of the hill, to the east of the palace, a small white-stone Church of the Annunciation was erected. Historically valuable portions of these ancient structures survive as parts of the buildings existing today.

Once again, in this period of great popular exertion and exultation in victory, the painters worked alongside the architects in embellishing the new churches. The most noted among them were Feofan Grek ("Theophanes the Greek") and Andrei Rublyov. The beautiful icons painted by them in 1405 for the iconostasis in the court Church of the Annunciation are the gems of the Kremlin collection. The vehement dramatism of Feofan's genius, so vividly manifested in his murals in Great Novgorod, is here mellowed to a sublime serenity. It was echoed in young Andrei Rublyov's radiant and soulful genius, which found expression in a number of brilliantly executed icons in the "festive" tier of the iconostasis. This iconostasis was a milestone in the history of monumental art in ancient Rus: it introduced an essential change in the interior of temples, separating the altar from the nave, equalising the worshippers and drawing them closer together in the presence of the deity and fostering their unity, which was so essential in the period of Moscow's rapid and turbulent rise.

The white-stoned Kremlin became a bastion and monumental symbol. The majesty and beauty of its architecture evoked the admiration of contemporaries and gave people confidence in their country's future. Enchanted by the creations of Russian architects, Feofan Grek painted a panorama of Moscow's Kremlin in two of his frescoes there.

In the 14th and 15th centuries, the Kremlin became the focal point of Russian culture. Moscow was not merely uniting Rus; it was bringing together her cultural heritage, selecting the best that the past had to offer. Moscow's architects developed the great traditions of the men who built the white-stone churches of Vladimir; the traditions of the painters of Rostov and Suzdal were enriched with the experience of Greek masters; the immortal spirit of the *Lay of Igor's Campaign* was revived in Rus letters, which sang paeans to the victory at Kulikovo. Chroniclers at the Metropolitan's court in the Kremlin developed the idea of Rus's unity, might and strength, showing that this was the trend of her entire history. The foundations of a national Russian culture were being laid at the Kremlin. Moscow itself had by that time spread well beyond the Kremlin's walls, becoming a large and populous city of merchants and artisans, with expanding economic ties with the whole of Rus and with foreign countries.

This brings us to the Kremlin's monuments of the 15th–17th centuries that have survived to our day. In his superb photographs Karel Neubert has found unexpected points of view and has caught new facets of their beauty. To follow him we must sometimes step aside from the measured tread of history and view a monument in all the complexity of its centuries of artistic life.

At the close of the 15th and beginning of the 16th century, the two hundred years of struggle to unify Rus culminated in the emergence of Europe's largest centralised state. Once again the Kremlin underwent a period of reconstruction, but on a scale, and with an ideological purpose, beyond the dreams of Kalita or Dmitry Donskoi. The dilapidated white walls of the Kremlin did not become the residence of the mighty "sovereign of all Rus" and of the All-Russian ecclesiastical centre—the white-stone churches and wooden palaces of an earlier age were much too small. Everything was built anew. But even in this leap forward, which seemed to make a clean break with the gloom of the Mongol invasion and the dismemberment of Russia, the link between the old and the new, between progress and hallowed tradition, between tradition and interest in the West was not only maintained but also emphasised. On the one hand, Italian engineers and architects worked side by side with leading Russian architects from Pskov, Tver, Rostov and Moscow itself; on the other, architects were sent to Vladimir and Novgorod to study famed churches of the past: the Cathedral of the Assumption in Vladimir was to be the model for a new cathedral in the Kremlin. The Kremlin's walls followed the old perimeter, with some deviation only in the north to give them more geometrical regularity, while the new churches were built on the sites of the old. The ancient pattern of the Kremlin ensemble was thus preserved, and the traditions of ancient Rus art were fused with the innovations of the Renaissance, brought in by Italian masters. Once again Russian painters, among them the refined Dionysius and his sons and assistants, worked in the Kremlin side by side with the architects.

The Kremlin's general fortifications were designed by the most prominent of the Italian architects invited to Moscow—Ridolfo Fioravante, of Bologna, who in Russia was called Aristotle for his extensive learning. Other architects worked on individual sectors of the fortress. In 1485–1487, Anthony Fryazin built the towers and walls of the southern side of the Kremlin; in 1490–1492, Pietro Antonio Solario worked on the eastern wall between the Beklemishevskaya and Nikolskaya towers. Lastly, the walls and towers of the most difficult western section along the swampy bank of the Neglinnaya, and the white-stone-faced moat with dams on the eastern side were built in 1494–1510 by the engineer Alevizo. The

Kremlin, with its 2.25 kilometres of crenellated battlements and 19 big towers, was surrounded by a moat and the Neglinnaya, whose water level was raised with dams. It was impossible to storm the fortress with assault ladders because of the high walls, protected by flanking fire from the towers. The gates with their drawbridges, barbicans, iron-bound oaken folds and iron portcullises were impregnable. If we imagine the towers without the 17th-century hip roofs we get a picture of the Kremlin in its original military sternness and regal beauty. The men who built it were skilled not only in the prose of military engineering but also in the poetry of architecture.

The Kremlin's walls on the inside, with their battle platforms and numerous archways, appeared to group and frame the diversified and picturesque ensemble within. The cathedral square with its golden-domed temples remained its centre.

The Cathedral of the Assumption (1474–1479), built by Aristotle Fioravante, now became the central cathedral of the Russian state. Regally majestic, it dominated the buildings around it. Its portals and arcature, features in the hallowed Vladimir tradition, emphasised the broad white smoothness of its symmetrical façades crowned with faced barrel vaults and a quintet of stately, gilded domes. Contemporaries were amazed to find the spacious, well-lit interior of the cathedral without the traditional choir gallery. It looked like a huge, festive hall, whose lofty vaulting rested on slender columns with leafed capitals. The cathedral's aerial breadth was accentuated by now non-existent frescoes dating from 1514. Fragments of frescoes (made by Dionysius and his school in about 1480) showing light, graceful figures and exquisitely harmonious compositions in delicate lilac, rose, blue and golden-yellow tones, have survived in the altar. Comparing the new edifice with Kalita's small church, the people of Moscow could visualise the tremendous progress that had been accomplished in Rus. The 16th and 17th centuries made their own contribution to the cathedral's treasure-store of art: the royal pew, with its whimsical tent-like canopy and a series of bas-reliefs, made by a Moscow engraver, illustrating the legend of the regalia of Moscow's rulers (1551), and a masterpiece by the founder Dmitry Sverchkov—a fretted copper reliquary over the "Lord's vestments"—set off the monumental grandeur of the temple with their ingenious ornamentation.

Almost adjoining the western façade of the Cathedral of the Assumption, Pskov architects built the small Rizopolozheniye Church (commemorating the Feast of the Laying of Our Lady's Vestments; 1485). Resting on a tall substructure, this small graceful building with its well-proportioned, modest façades emphasised the imperious majesty of its neighbour and, at the same time, lent intimacy and warmth to this corner of the Kremlin ensemble. The Cathedral of the Annunciation (1485), built by the same Pskov architects, originally had three domes and towered to advantage over an open stone platform which included the substructure of a 14th-century white-stone church. It was connected with the palace by a passage, and had the traditional gallery for the prince's family. It was closely linked with Russian traditions in architecture, evident in the cupola resting on a pedestal covered with rounded panels, the arcature, and the ogee vaults; the handsome jasper tile floor was brought from Rostov Cathedral, and the resplendent gates "done in gold" (16th century) were made in the style of the famed "golden gates" of the 12th-13th-century cathedrals of Vladimir and Suzdal. The paintings of the iconostasis, by Feofan Grek and Rublyov, were echoed in frescoes (1508, by Feodosy, the son of Dionysius, and assistants), where a prominent place was occupied by the themes of the Apocalypse and the Last Judgment and a cycle portraying Byzantine and Rus rulers, as a reflection of the theory that Moscow's rulers were in the line of succession to those of Byzantium. The artistic style of the frescoes, which were akin in spirit to those of Dionysius but were not quite so monumental, approximated to icon paintings, although their tones were brighter and more solid. The painters, who saw the Kremlin built, made wide use of architectural elements in their compositions. The cathedral changed in silhouette with the addition in the 16th century of small chapels (1564) on the corners of its podium, and two more cupolas, which brought up the total of its domes to nine and made the pile unusually picturesque.

Aleviz Novy (Alevisio the Later) likewise used an old site for his grand Cathedral of the Archangel Michael (1505–1508), the burial-place of Moscow princes and tsars. There was nothing sombre about this mausoleum; the impression was that the architect had sought to assert the triumph of life over death. He dressed the traditional five-domed cathedral in magnificent and gay Renaissance attire, adorning its façades with decorative motifs from Venetian architecture. The tomb looked more like a rich two-storeyed palace with a striking loggia, slender Corinthian pilasters and cornices and succulent shells on the barrel vault facing. Only separate fragments remain of the original painting (made in about 1509): the murals as a whole were made in 1652–1666 by skilled artists of the Armoury. They created a gallery of "portraits" of Russian princes from Vladimir I to Vasily III, who built the cathedral, showing their heroes in the ornate costumes of the 17th century; on the southern and northern walls they gave a monumental account of the miracles performed by the Archangel Michael, with numerous battle scenes. The murals of the mausoleum perpetuated the memory of the rulers of Rus and asserted the invincibility of their arms. The solemn white tombstones with the delicate carvings and inscriptions on them were made by Russian craftsmen in 1636–1637.

The old palace was pulled down and replaced by a vast complex of stone buildings on high vaulted substructures (1492–1508). Prominent among these was the Granovitaya Palata (Faceted Hall), built in 1487–1491 by Pietro Solario in the style of similar Russian buildings in Novgorod and the Troitse-Sergiev Monastery. Church hierarchs were consecrated in this stately, well-lit, single-pillared hall, which was also used as an audience chamber and for the sittings of the state assembly. It faced the cathedral square. The murals (end of the 16th century), of which we know from descriptions, were devoted to edifying themes from the Bible and Russian history.

All these buildings were dominated by the Ivan the Great belfry, a mighty, faceted "pillar" (1505–1508; architect, Fryazin), which developed in stone the popular log tower church. A belfry (1532–1543; architect, Petroche the Little) was added to the "pillar" for a new peal of bells, whose mighty carillon could be heard for miles around. In 1600, the height of this "pillar" was raised to 80 metres. Standing in the centre of the Kremlin it became its most prominent landmark. This giant in its cap of gold harmonised the Kremlin temples with their gilded domes into a proud architectural symphony, which seemed to reaffirm in stone the idea of the supreme centralising force of the reigning city of Moscow. The ensemble of the cathedral square, facing the river and reflected in it, was the Kremlin's chief façade; the builders strove to show as much of its panorama as was possible, and so the opposite bank of the Moskva and of the Neglinnaya was cleared of buildings.

The rôle of the Kremlin as the seat of Russian culture and art was still further enhanced in the 15th and 16th centuries. Moscow tirelessly continued to collect the cultural wealth of the past, concentrating it in the Kremlin and adding to it new works by new masters. Outstanding ancient paintings and the best icons from different art centres of Rus were collected in the Kremlin cathedrals and churches. Built in 1511, the Armoury, initially a depository of the royal arms and armour, later became a museum of applied art. Ancient manuscripts were collected in the Kremlin, and in it were written such colossal works as the Great Euchology and Martyrology (a many-tomed encyclopedia of the Russian church). Such literary monuments matched the giants of the Kremlin's architecture.

The church lost its dominating rôle in the spiritual life of the people when laymen-artists of popular origin began to be increasingly concerned with developing Russian culture. Secular principles gained ground. Dionysius, the great artist of "regal Moscow", was not a monk but a layman. A secular spirit, the breath of life itself, pervaded the temples of the Kremlin. The city grew rapidly. It was ringed with the new walls of Kitai-Gorod, which adjoined the Kremlin (1534–1537; architect, Petroche the Little) and the giant circle of the White City (1586–1593; architect, Fyodor Kon). In 1555–1560, a memorial to the victory over the Kazan Khanate—the fabulous Cathedral of the Intercession, better known as St. Basil's Cathedral—was erected near the Kremlin, in the market-square. The question of who built it remains debatable: it may have been built by two Russian architects, Barma and Postnik (Faster) Yakovlev, or by one, Postnik Barma, son of Yakov. Its fantastic, jubilant beauty is in striking contrast to the sternness of the Kremlin fortress and the stately serenity of its temples.

Russian culture became more and more worldly after the grim trials of the war early in the 17th century, when the foreign invaders were driven out of Moscow and Russia, and when the people stepped into the limelight with formidable peasant revolts and subsequent urban uprisings.

The dam which had held art within the narrow bounds of the Church and the feudal court was breached in the 17th century: hundreds of painters, sculptors and architects, many of whom won lasting fame, came from the towns and villages of Russia. Popular taste was largely reflected in the preference for flowery decoration in architecture, entertaining narrative in prose, and festive tones and intricate patterns in painting. This tendency was also pronounced in the Kremlin's monuments.

In 1624–1625, a triumphal canopy (architects, Bazhen Ogurtsov and Christopher Galloway) was erected over the Spasskaya Tower, which faces St. Basil's Cathedral and the old market-square. It combined the Russian tier composition with fanciful Gothic details. Later, in 1672–1686, the other towers were also surmounted with graceful tiered canopies. The Kremlin gradually shed its military sternness and, as though vying with the ornate St. Basil's Cathedral, acquired the character of a fairy-tale city straight out of Russian folklore. The superstructures of the towers almost doubled their height and the Kremlin again dominated the panorama of the now far-flung city of Moscow.

New buildings continued to appear in the Kremlin almost uninterruptedly.

The Teremnoy (Belvedere) Palace (1635–1636; architects, Ogurtsov and associates) was erected on old 16th-century substructures. Its tiered composition and its open promenade balconies harmonised with the tiered tops of the Kremlin's towers, a gilded watch-tower dominating the rambling pile. The façade with its rows of bright windows, engraved white-stone platbands, elaborate cornices and string courses of brilliant coloured tiles breathed a refreshing *joie de vivre*. There is an air of warm comfort about the cosy rooms, which were rather small, with their fanciful engravings on white stone, the beautiful shimmering tiles of the stoves and the inexhaustible inventiveness of the ornamental design on the walls and vaults (the present paintings were made in the 19th century). Work on the palace buildings continued until the 1680s, when in their midst there arose the new court Verkhospassky Church with a group of gilded domes resting on slender tiled shafts; beside the majestic domes of the Cathedral of the Assumption they sound as a tremulous chime amid the mighty boom of the huge Tsar Bell.

Adjoining the Teremnoy Palace by the Kremlin's western wall rose the mansion of the boyar Miloslavsky. In 1672, it was turned into the royal Poteshny (Amusement) Palace, where Russia's first theatrical performances were staged. The huge machicolations of the façade supporting the altar of the private chapel create an effective contrast to the fine carving of the details.

Like the royal palace, the Patriarch's palace, which stood to the north of the Cathedral of the Assumption, underwent considerable reconstruction (1652–1656), but in contrast to the richly decorated royal premises its private Church of the Twelve Apostles was deliberately austere and followed the pattern of ancient churches with their arcatures and monumental ensembles of five domes. Krestovaya Palata, the Metropolitan's audience hall, which vied with the royal Faceted Hall in size and was boldly ceilinged by a coved vault, evoked the admiration of contemporaries.

In the 17th century, the Kremlin set the tone in art and culture. Its architectural style was echoed in the architecture of Russian towns and monasteries. The Armoury and the other Kremlin workshops became a kind of "Academy of Arts" for Rus, employing people skilled in various branches of applied art as well as prominent artists. Among these was Simon Ushakov, precursor of Russian realistic painting, who directed all the decorative work in the Kremlin. During the war with Sweden, the Kremlin's fortifications were reinforced, and the big Arsenal (1702–1736; architect, D. Ivanov) was built in its north-western corner. Peter the Great celebrated the victory at Poltava (1709) in the Kremlin's Faceted Hall, thereby giving regal Moscow a parting token of homage; in 1713 St. Petersburg became Russia's capital, and all building in the Kremlin ceased.

The 18th century was a difficult period for the Kremlin. Its fate depended on the whims of the imperial court, which did not appreciate its national importance. Acting on impulse, Catherine II ordered a huge palace to be built in the Kremlin under the direction of the celebrated architect Vasily Bazhenov. A part of the Kremlin's southern wall was pulled down to make room for the enormous edifice, more than 600 metres long with numerous columns, which would have hidden from view the ancient ensemble of the cathedral square. Fortunately for Russian culture, the palace was never built, and the Kremlin wall and towers were restored (1775–1783).

Mikhail Kazakov, a pupil of Bazhenov's and a prominent exponent of Russian classicism, had the difficult task of erecting a large public building, the Senate (1776–1788). Appreciating the importance of the Kremlin's ancient architecture, he ingeniously incorporated his creation into it. The light-flooded round state-room of the Senate with its graceful Corinthian columns and giant coffered cupola (the height of the hall is 27 metres, and the span of the cupola 24.7 metres) was a real masterpiece, and contemporaries justly called it the Russian Pantheon.

The trying but glorious year 1812, which witnessed the defeat of Napoleon's army, brought great destruction to the Kremlin. Before fleeing from Moscow, the "Ruler of the World" ordered the Kremlin to be blown up. But heroic Muscovites foiled the intentions of the imperial Vandal: only a few of the ancient buildings and towers were badly wrecked by the explosions. Their restoration (1814–1835) was entrusted to the leading architects of the day (Bovet, Rossi and Gilardi).

The ageing palaces of the Moscow tsars were not restored. Nicholas I ordered a new palace to be built on their site, incorporating parts of ancient buildings (1839–1849). The Armoury (1844–1851) was erected on Kremlin Hill. Academician K. A. Ton, who designed these buildings, was the founder of an eclectic pseudo-Russian style embracing Byzantine, ancient Russian and classical motifs, the style which received "royal approval". The design on the façades imitated the form of the windows and decorative motifs of the Teremnoy Palace, while the arcade of the ground floor linked this unimaginative and inartistic building, so alien to the Kremlin's architecture, with the Cathedral of the Annunciation on its flank. The second floor contained a number of huge, ostentatious halls decorated with extravagant and depressing lavishness.

Moscow again became the country's capital after the Great October Socialist Revolution. The Soviet Government established itself in the Kremlin on March 11, 1918. Lenin showed great solicitude for the Kremlin's monuments and organised their protection and restoration.

Scientists, artists and architects have made extensive studies to discover the true value of the Kremlin art treasures and it is now a great museum of Russian culture. The austere, magnificent Lenin Mausoleum (1929–1930; architect, Academician A. V. Shchusev) was erected beyond the Kremlin's eastern wall, where silver firs form a canopy over the graves of prominent leaders of the Revolution and the Soviet State.

However, the growing requirements of the government centre of the young Socialist state made necessary considerable reconstruction of the Kremlin. This was a natural process; at each stage old buildings were replaced by new ones, changing its face. In recent years, as well, some of its old buildings had to make way. The Chudov and Voznesenye (Ascension) monasteries at the Spassky Gates were replaced by a government building (1932–1934; architect, I. I. Rehrberg), which considerably enlarged the cathedral square. Ton's palace was remodelled; two of its halls were merged into one vast impressive hall, in which the Supreme Soviet of the U.S.S.R. used to hold its sessions (architect, I. A. Ivanov-Schietz).

In 1961, Soviet architects built the large new Palace of Congresses (chief architect, M. V. Posokhin). The choice of the site north of the Teremnoy Palace made it possible to avoid considerable inroads into the old composition; the lower levels of the building were sunk deep into Kremlin Hill, to prevent its silhouette from obscuring the ancient panorama of the Kremlin. Only its western façade is seen above the walls and this strikes a balance with the upper storeys of the Arsenal rising to the north. Its architects made no attempt to imitate ancient traditions or mask the Palace in old forms. A giant crystal, bright and light, it is in clear contrast with the buildings of ages long past, boldly asserting the new beside the old and forming a bridge between the past and the future.

3

WALLS AND TOWERS

5

9

13

16

17

18

21

ANCIENT PAINTINGS AND ARCHITECTURE

24

28

31

32

33

34

35

37

41

42

44

45

48

50

51

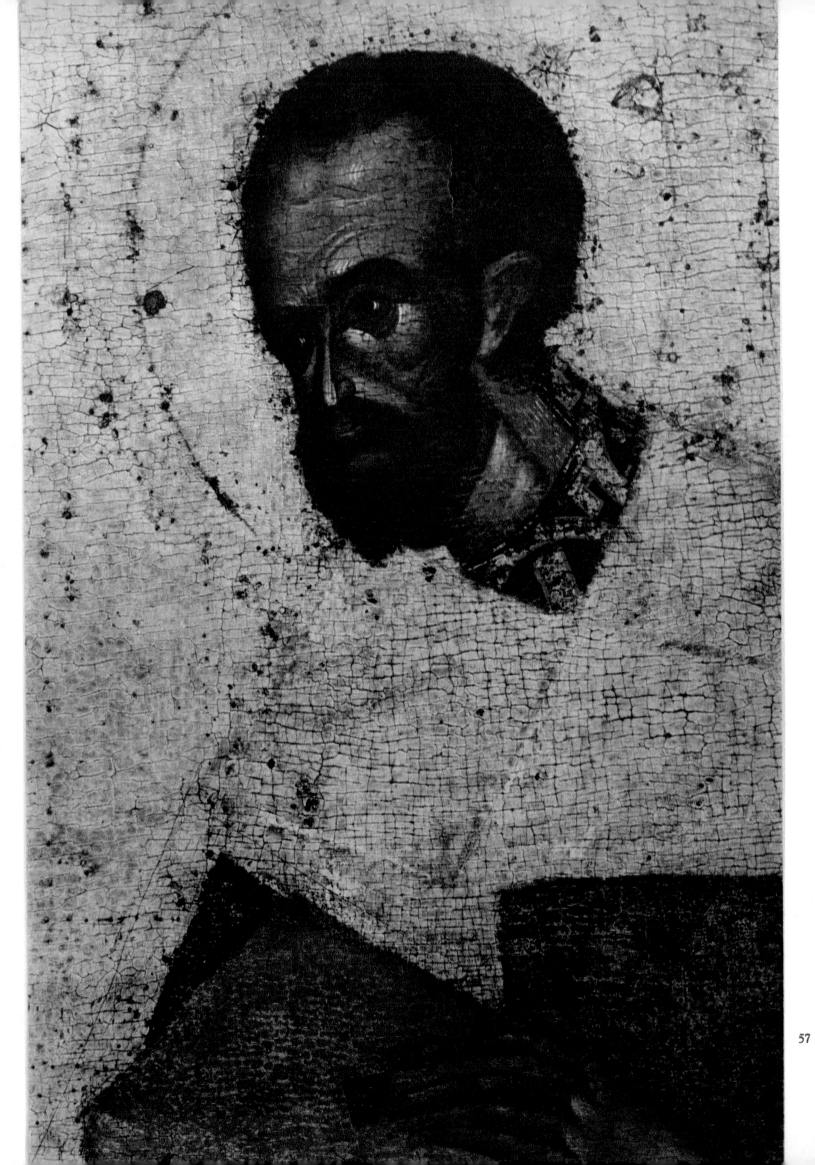

58

59

63

64

65

71

73

79

80

81

83

PALACES

84

87

88

91

93

97

100

101

103

106

109

110

PUBLIC BUILDINGS
AND MONUMENTS

111

113

114

118

119

122

123

I WALLS AND TOWERS

1, 14, 15. BEKLEMISHEVSKAYA TOWER was built by Anthony Fryazin in 1487 and got its name from the nearby bailey of the boyar Beklemishev. Its graceful outline was enhanced by the slender tapering canopy erected in the late 17th century.

2. VIEW OF THE KREMLIN AND THE MOSKVA RIVER

3, 5. SPASSKAYA TOWER, 71 metres high, as seen from inside the Kremlin, of which it is the main gateway. The original tower was built by Pietro Antonio Solario in 1491. The tiered top, curiously ornamented in white stone, was added by Bazhen Ogurtsov in 1626–1628. The clockwork which sounds the peal was installed by Christopher Galloway. Its chimes are heard on Moscow Radio's home service at 6 a.m. and midnight. A five-pointed ruby star, 3.75 metres across, was mounted on the pinnacle in 1936 and remodelled in 1946. To the right are the small "Tsarskaya Tower" and the great "Nabatnaya (Tocsin) Tower".

4. RED SQUARE. THE LENIN MAUSOLEUM. The Lenin Mausoleum was designed by A. V. Shchusev and erected in 1924 at the foot of the Kremlin's Senate Tower. In 1929–1930, the temporary woodwork structure was replaced by the granite and labrador mausoleum. It also serves as a stand from which the leaders of the Communist Party and the Soviet Government review holiday demonstrations and parades. Behind it, along the Kremlin wall, is a necropolis of prominent revolutionaries and Party and Government leaders. In the distance is Spasskaya Tower, and beyond the Senate Tower is seen the dome, with flag flying, of the building housing the Council of Ministers of the U.S.S.R.

5. SPASSKAYA TOWER (see note on Plate 3)

6. NIKOLSKAYA TOWER, 60.2 metres high, was named after the icon of St. Nicolai, the Miracle-worker, which used to hang above its gateway. It was built in 1492 by Pietro Antonio Solario and was destroyed by Napoleon's retreating troops in 1812. In 1816, it was restored by A. Bakharev, who decorated it with rich carvings in white stone and erected a tiered octagonal top surmounted with a canopy. The ruby star was installed in 1937.

7. NORTH-WEST ARSENAL CORNER TOWER was built in 1492 by Pietro Antonio Solario, and the canopied top was added in the 1670s. Beyond the tower is the Arsenal; in the distance are Nikolskaya and Spasskaya Towers facing Red Square.

8. KUTAFIA AND TROITSKAYA TOWERS. In the foreground is Kutafia Tower, built in the 16th century as a tête-de-pont, its name being the colloquial for "clumsy, muffled up woman". It got its broad arched gateway and decorative Moscow Baroque arcade in the late 17th century. The bridge leading from Kutafia Tower to Troitsky Gateway across the Neglinnaya River (now running in a subterranean sewer below Alexandrovsky Gardens) was first built in the 16th century but fell into disrepair and was completely rebuilt in 1901.

9. TROITSKAYA TOWER, 80 metres high, and GATEWAY seen from inside the Kremlin. Its name derives from the inn of the Troitsky Monastery in the Kremlin. The tower dates to 1495 and its tiered and canopied top to 1685; it is decorated with white stone carvings much like those of Spasskaya Tower. Its ruby star was mounted in 1937.

10. BOROVITSKAYA TOWER, 54.5 metres high, and GATEWAY. It was designed and built by Alevizo in 1494. Etymologically its name (bor=pine forest) is a topographical clue: in the old days Kremlin Hill was clothed in a forest of pines. Unlike the other Kremlin towers it has a side structure with openings for the chains used to operate the drawbridge across the Neglinnaya. The tiered canopied top was erected in the late 17th century; the star in 1937.

11. A VIEW OF THE KREMLIN from beyond the Moskva River to the south-east, one of its most beautiful prospects: the belt of walls rhythmically spaced with towers, the clear-cut silhouette of the cathedrals and the campanile, and the solid bulk of the palace and government buildings.

12. THE KREMLIN'S SOUTH WALL AND TOWERS ALONG THE MOSKVA RIVER. Towers left to right are: Vodovzvod-

naya, Blagoveshchenskaya, the canopy of Borovitskaya, Tainitskaya, First and Second Bezymyannaya, and Petrovskaya. All were built in 1485 by Anthony Fryazin, and surmounted by decorative canopies in the late 17th century. In the 1770s, a part of the walls and towers were dismantled to make way for the projected Grand Kremlin Palace designed by Vasily Bazhenov. When the project was abandoned, the whole was restored to its original form.

13. TAINITSKAYA TOWER, seen from inside the Kremlin. It was built by Anthony Fryazin in 1485 and initially had a gateway. Its name (*taina*=secret) suggests that it served as a secret water reservoir and may have had a passage leading to the Moskva River. Like other towers, it was surmounted by a decorative top with an observation tower at the end of the 17th century.

14, 15. BEKLEMISHEVSKAYA TOWER (see note on Plate 1)

16. TSARSKAYA TOWER was built on top of the Kremlin wall close by Spasskaya Tower in 1680, and was a sort of belvedere from which the tsars watched events in Red Square.

17. THE KREMLIN SOUTH-EAST WALL AND TOWERS between the corner Beklemishevskaya Tower and Spasskaya Tower Gateway. Towers left to right are: Beklemishevskaya, Konstantino-Yeleninskaya, Nabatnaya, Tsarskaya, and Spasskaya. Depending on the lie of the land, the Kremlin wall, 2,235 metres long, is from 5 to 9 metres high.

18. RED SQUARE, as seen from the Moskva River. Towers to the left are: Konstantino-Yeleninskaya, Nabatnaya and Spasskaya; to the right is St. Basil's Cathedral.

19. ST. BASIL'S CATHEDRAL in Red Square. It stands near the Spasskaya Tower Gateway to the Kremlin and was built in 1555–1560 by Barma and "Faster" Yakovlev (according to another reading of the ancient inscription there was only one architect: "Faster" Barma, son of Yakov). It is a unique monument of old Russian architecture. The well-proportioned pyramidal pile is made up of nine campaniles, each with an architectural character of its own. It commemorates the victory over the Kazan Khanate. In the 17th century, the open platform on which the campaniles stood was vaulted and the whole richly painted. In front of the cathedral is the sculptured monument by I. Martos (1818) to Minin and Pozharsky, who led the people against the invader in the early 17th century.

20. VODOVZVODNAYA CORNER TOWER of the Kremlin, 61.85 metres high, was built by Anthony Fryazin in 1489. In the 17th century, the tower housed a mechanism for piping water into the palaces and gardens. It was blown up by Napoleon's retreating troops in 1812 and restored in 1817–1819 by O. I. Bovet. The ruby star dates to 1937.

II ANCIENT PAINTINGS AND ARCHITECTURE

21. CUPOLAS OF THE TEREMNOY CHAPELS (see note on Plate 110)

22–23. PORTAL AND INTERIOR OF THE CHURCH OF THE NATIVITY OF OUR LADY (A CHANTRY OF THE RESURRECTION OF LAZARUS). It was erected in 1393, and remodelled in the 16th and 17th centuries. In the 1840s, during the construction of the Grand Kremlin Palace, its layout was altered, and its walls plastered and painted with frescoes imitating ancient motifs. In the 1920s, the plasterwork of the 1840s was removed, revealing the original masonry of large white-stone blocks, a portal with ogee archivolts, an intermural staircase and other details. The church is one of the few relics of the white stone architecture of old Moscow.

24–25. CATHEDRAL OF THE ASSUMPTION, seen from the south and from above. It was built by Aristotle Fioravante in 1474–1479 on the site of a cathedral of 1326. It has white stone walls, brick vaults and drums surmounted with gilt-copper cupolas. The south, north and west portals and tympanums are painted with 17th-century frescoes.

This was the chief temple of Ancient Rus, the place of coronation ceremonies and promulgation of acts of state. It contains the tombs of the Moscow Metropolitans and Patriarchs (the last in 1700). It is now a very popular museum of history and art. Restoration work has revealed some remarkable murals and canvases dating from between the 12th and the 17th centuries.

26. ICONOSTASIS AND MURALS IN THE CATHEDRAL OF THE ASSUMPTION. Most of the murals were painted in 1642–1643, when almost all the earlier frescoes were removed by order of Tsar Alexei Mikhailovich, and replaced by new ones (some compositions dating to about 1480 have been preserved in the altar). The 17th-century murals were done by a large group of artists and assistants, more than a hundred all told. They were headed by the leading royal iconographers Ivan and Boris Pasein, Sidor Pospeyev, Mark Matveyev, Bazhen Savin, and image painters from other towns, Ivan Muravei of Nizhny Novgorod and Lubim Ageyev, and Vasily Ilyin of Kostroma. The subjects are as follows: inside the five cupolas are God the Father, God the Son (as Christ the Almighty, a Veronica image of Christ, and Christ Emmanuel), Our Lady, the angels, the patriarchs and the prophets; on the curved inner surfaces of the vaults are legends from the Gospel; on the pillars and tali, the saints, among them Russian princes; on the walls, scenes from the Gospel, subjects taken from the Book in Praise of Our Lady; Ecumenical Councils, and the Last Judgement; in the altar is the Liturgy.

The present iconostasis (the original one has not been preserved) consists of five tiers of icons, the top four painted and decorated with chased silver trimmings in 1652. In the lower row and over the side-doors are the very old icons of the 12th, 13th, 14th and 15th centuries, painted in Moscow for the Kremlin cathedrals, and also some brought by the Moscow princes and tsars from other art centres of ancient Rus.

27. CATHEDRAL OF THE ASSUMPTION, a view from below of the central drum, the vaulting and the dome. All the drums have the same internal diameter, but on the outside the central one is much larger. They are supported by round pillars, which in the 15th century were surmounted by capitals, called "timbers" by the chronicler. The cross-vaults are notable for the first use of iron braces in Russian architecture. The 17th-century frescoes were retouched in the 1910s.

28. ST. JOHN CHRYSOSTOM, ST. BASIL THE GREAT, ST. GREGORY THE DIVINE. Detail from the liturgical composition, The Great Issue. This is a mural dating to 1642–1643 in the apse of the bema of the Cathedral of the Assumption, executed in tempera on a fresco background, and recovered in 1960 from additions and 18th and 19th-century superimpositions.

29. ADORATION OF THE MAGI. A fresco (about 1480) on the north wall of the Pokhvalsky Chantry of the Cathedral of the Assumption. Painted by Dionysius, an outstanding exponent of the Moscow school of the late 15th and early 16th century.

The chronicler tells us that when the Cathedral of the Assumption was built only its bema was decorated, the walls, vaulting and pillars in the nave remaining unadorned until 1513–1514.

The altar frescoes of the Pokhvalsky Chantry are ascribed to Dionysius because in style and manner of execution they are remarkably similar to the 1500–1502 frescoes in the Cathedral of Ferapontov Monastery, where his authorship has been well established.

The painter of the Adoration of the Magi in the Pokhvalsky Chantry made skilful use of the wall space with its rounded top, the composition deriving its harmony from the flowing rhythm of the plastic outlines of the bowed, almost ethereal, forms.

30. MOTHER OF GOD. Detail from a fresco "Glory be to the Mother of God", on the vaulted surface of the Pokhvalsky Chantry in the bema of the Cathedral of the Assumption. Done by Dionysius in about 1480.

A soft radiance seems to emanate from the face of the Mother of God. It is a fine specimen of Dionysius's style: soft flowing lines and a delicate blend of colours.

31. ST. GEORGE THE VICTORIOUS (on the back is a 12th-century icon, *Stella Maris*). This is one of the oldest icons in the Moscow Kremlin. The image of St. George is an embodiment of the popular ideal of military valour as sung in *The Lay of Igor's Campaign*, the famous epic poem of the late 12th century.

Because the original painting on the back has not been preserved all over, a superimposed 14th-century painting has been allowed to remain.

Wood, canvas, gesso, tempera. Size 168 × 121 cm.

Discovered in the iconostasis of the Cathedral of the Assumption.

32. OUR LORD OF THE GOLDEN HAIR. An icon dating from the early 13th century. It does not derive its title from any iconographic canon, but from the golden colour of Christ's hair.

The majestic image of Christ, with fine features and rich imaginative ornamentation, is highly characteristic of the school of the Vladimir-Suzdal Principality, of which Moscow was a frontier citadel.

Wood, canvas, gesso, tempera. Size 58 × 42 cm.

Discovered over the north doorway of the iconostasis of the Cathedral of the Assumption (now on display in the Chrism Chamber).

33. THE APPARITION OF MICHAEL THE ARCHANGEL TO JOSHUA, an icon of the early 13th century, Vladimir-Suzdal school. It may have been painted for the ancient wooden Church of Michael the Archangel, built in the Kremlin in the 12th or 13th century.

In Rus, the Archangel Michael, the Commander-in-Chief of the celestial host, was the princes' patron saint in war. The biblical Joshua (the small crouching figure at the Archangel's feet) is here depicted as a Russian prince.

The graceful and majestic Archangel, armed in all his celestial panoply, copiously adorned with patterns of gold, is a typical work of the Vladimir-Suzdal school of the pre-Mongol era.

Wood, canvas, gesso, tempera. Size 50 × 35 cm.

Formerly in the Cathedral of the Assumption (now on display in the Chrism Chamber.)

34. THE CHASTENING EYE OF THE LORD, an icon dating to the 1340s, was presumably made by one of the Greek artists or by one of their Moscow pupils who in 1344 decorated the old Cathedral of the Assumption, which until 1472 stood on the site of the present one in the Kremlin.

The Chastening Eye of the Lord is the name by which the icon was known among the people. It reflects the medieval artist's idea of God as the strict chastiser sitting in judgment on the world.

Wood, canvas, gesso, tempera. Size 100 × 77 cm.

Over the south doorway of the iconostasis of the Cathedral of the Assumption.

35. ANGEL. Detail from the icon *Old Testament Trinity*, dating from the first half of the 14th century. It may have been painted in Moscow, in the traditional style of the Vladimir-Suzdal school, for the old (1326) Cathedral of the Assumption. The original icon lies under several paintings superimposed in the course of the centuries, and a very dark layer of drying oil. Partial removals in 1946 revealed an excellent ancient icon in a very good state of preservation.

36. THE APOSTLE PAUL. Detail from the icon *The Apostles Peter and Paul*, painted by a Greek painter in the late 14th century. Only a part of Paul's figure has been cleared of later retouching and old drying oil.

Wood, canvas, gesso, tempera. Size 196 × 137 cm.

On the south wall of the Cathedral of the Assumption.

37. OUR LADY OF VLADIMIR, an icon dating from the early 15th century, by a painter of Rublyov's circle.

It was believed to be a copy of an icon of the same name, which was very popular and much revered in ancient Rus. The original was by an unknown Byzantine artist of the 11th or 12th century, and was brought to Kiev in the 12th century; in 1155 it was taken to Vladimir, and in the 15th century, on to Moscow, where it was placed in the Cathedral of the Assumption (at present on display at the Tretyakov State Gallery). In those days a copy was not meant to be a faithful reproduction of the original, and so while the early 15th-century icon more or less imitates the Byzantine model iconographically, the character of its image and the interpretation are quite different. The original, which came closer to pictorial illusionism, was the image of a dolorous Our Lady; the copy, in a more generalised linear manner, is the picture of gracious and serene femininity.

Wood, canvas, gesso, tempera. Size 105 × 67 cm.

In the image case by the Holy Doors of the Cathedral of the Assumption.

38. IN THEE REJOICE. An icon of the 1480s by an artist of Dionysius's circle.

An illustration of the hymn in praise of the Mother of God intoned by the angels and the human race. The words are written on a scroll in the hands of the author, the 8th-century Byzantine theologian John Damascene, who is portrayed at the feet of the enthroned Mother of God. The whole is a splendid expression of the festive intonation of the joyous canticle.

Wood, canvas, gesso, tempera. Size 200 × 155 cm.

In the iconostasis of the Cathedral of the Assumption.

39. DETAIL FROM THE APOCALYPSE, an icon dating from the late 15th or early 16th century, by a painter of Dionysius's circle. The composition illustrates the fantastic visions in the Apocalypse about the end of the world, the Last Judgment, the punishment of the wicked, and Christ's war against the dark forces of hell. But Dionysius, who painted the Apocalypse for the Cathedral of the Assumption in the Kremlin, did not adopt the sombre mysticism of the Apocalypse. He illustrated it in masterly images radiating triumphant justice. The whole is a festively ornate arrangement of light, graceful forms.

Wood, canvas, gesso, tempera. Size 185 × 151 cm.

On the west wall of the Cathedral of the Assumption.

40. METROPOLITAN PYOTR AND HIS LIFE, an icon by Dionysius. Late 15th or early 16th century.

The Metropolitan Pyotr was a prominent churchman and statesman in Muscovite Rus (the date of his birth is not known; he died in 1326). He was also something of an artist.

The panels around the large figure of the Metropolitan illustrate scenes from his life.

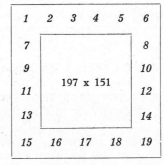

4. *Pyotr is ordained deacon.*

5. *Pyotr paints an icon.*

6. *Pyotr before the gate of the monastery he founded on the Ratj River.*

7. *Pyotr makes a present to the Metropolitan Maxim of an icon he painted.*

8. *Prince Yuri Galitsky entreats Pyotr to go to Constantinople to be consecrated Metropolitan of Kiev.*

1. *Pyotr's mother sees a prophetic dream.*

9. *Pyotr and his party sailing for Constantinople.*

2. *Pyotr is sent to a monastery for his schooling.*

10. *Pyotr with the Patriarch of Constantinople.*

3. *Pyotr becomes a monk.*

11. *The Patriarch consecrates*

Pyotr Metropolitan of all Rus (1305).

12. Pyotr at the Council of Pereyaslavl-Zalessky. He pardons the disgraced Bishop Andrei of Tver (1311).

13. Pyotr and builders lay the corner-stone of the Cathedral of the Assumption in the Moscow Kremlin (1326).

14. The Moscow Prince Ivan Kalita sees himself in a dream riding with the Metropolitan

Pyotr past a high mountain capped with thawing snow.

15. An angel announces to Pyotr the approach of his death.

16. From his throne the dying Pyotr admonishes the people.

17. As Pyotr's body is borne along, one who denies his sainthood has a vision of the seated Pyotr blessing the people.

18. Pyotr's interment.

19. The opening of Pyotr's relics.

Although the panels are small, they are done in a monumental style: the outlines of the light, graceful figures are generalised, all movement and gesture is serene, flowing and rhythmical. The colour scheme is typical of Dionysius, being produced by a very finely graded arrangement of dark and light tone stains.

Wood, canvas, gesso, tempera. Size 197 × 151 cm.

On the south wall of the Cathedral of the Assumption.

41. METROPOLITAN PYOTR LAYING THE CORNER-STONE OF THE CATHEDRAL OF THE ASSUMPTION AND OF HIS OWN TOMB. Detail from the icon *Metropolitan Pyotr and His Life.*

42. METROPOLITAN PYOTR AND THE MOSCOW PRINCE IVAN KALITA ON HORSEBACK. Detail from the icon *Metropolitan Pyotr and His Life.*

An illustration of the prophetic dream of Prince Ivan Kalita, in which he saw Metropolitan Pyotr and himself riding past a high mountain with a cap of thawing snow. This, the Metropolitan explained, augured greater power for the Prince and approaching death for himself.

43–45. THE ROYAL PEW IN THE CATHEDRAL OF THE ASSUMPTION was fashioned by Russian master-carvers for Tsar Ivan IV (the Terrible) in 1551. It was made of basswood and was gilded and painted. The canopy was highly popular in ancient Russian architecture, and here is one decorated with ogee finials, arrow-shaped frontals and an elaborate pattern of flowers and runners. Carvings on the walls depict 12 scenes from the Thracian campaigns of Prince Vladimir Monomakh of Kiev in the 11th century, and the legend of the presentation to him by the Emperor Constantine of Byzantium of royal regalia, as a mark of recognition that the Russian tsars were successors to the Byzantine Emperors.

46. THE SOUTH DOOR OF THE CATHEDRAL OF THE ASSUMPTION, whose massive copper panels are divided by ornamented strips into rectangles portraying religious scenes. The door was made in the late 15th century, in imitation of the 13th-century door at Suzdal, with the use of a special technique of fired gilding. The background is covered with a velvety jet-black lacquer, on which the drawing is done in mercurial gold. When heated, the gold and the copper formed a stable alloy, while the mercury evaporated. The soft incandescence of the gold against the black creates a remarkable effect. Objets d'art made with the use of this method were popular from the 12th to the 16th century.

47. BRONZE CANOPY in the south-west corner of the Cathedral of the Assumption. Cast in 1625 by Dmitry Sverchkov, it was initially designed as a reliquary. It is surrounded by a grille consisting of handsomely interwoven stalks and flowers and has a roof of copper sheets.

48. CHURCH OF THE LAYING OF OUR LADY'S VESTMENTS was built by Pskov architects in 1485–1486, as the private chapel of the Moscow Metropolitan. It stands on a high crypt and is surrounded by a podium reached by open staircases. The blind ogee arches topping the walls are in the style of the period. The drum of the cupola rests on platforms. A staircase connects the Cathedral with chapels and ancient chambers in the palace. The interior of the temple was decorated with frescoes in 1644. The icons were painted in 1627 by a team of iconographers led by Nazary Istomin.

49–52. THE CATHEDRAL OF THE ANNUNCIATION was built by Pskov architects in 1485–1489, as a private chapel for the Moscow princes. Chantries were erected at its four ends in 1564, and the south porch in 1572 (Plate 50). The 15th-century south portal was restored in 1950 (Plate 51). It is made of white stone, and has the characteristic ogee archivolt and capitals in the form of bound sheaves. The ornate west (Plate 52) and north portals were built in the 1560s in the style of the portals of the Cathedral of the Archangel.

53. INTERIOR VIEW OF THE CATHEDRAL OF THE ANNUNCIATION WITH MURALS AND ICONOSTASIS.

The murals were done in 1508 by Feodosy, son of Dionysius, and "brethren" (a team of painters).

The content of the murals and the arrangement of the various compositions on the inner surfaces of the vaulting, the walls and pillars of the temple on the whole follow the traditional canon. Special features here are the numerous scenes from the Apocalypse and the many images of Byzantine emperors and Russian princes. Later impositions were removed in the restoration work of 1947 and 1961. Bits of 18th and late 19th-century painting, imitating the ancient style, were left in the several places where the original has not been preserved.

The iconostasis was a partition between the bema and the nave. The icons on it were arranged in rows in strict accordance with the accepted order prevailing in Rus at the end of the 14th century. The lower, "local", row contained icons most revered in the particular temple. Above that, in the centre, was Christ the King, surrounded by the devout figures of the Mother of God, St. John the Baptist, the Archangels, the Apostles and other saints, depicted in supplication of Christ's forgiveness of the sins of men. Above that was a row of smaller icons portraying the "feasts", and higher up, a row of images of the prophets. Later additions contained the images of the patriarchs (16th century) and the Passion of Our Lord (17th century).

The icons of the second and third tiers (Christ the King, and the Feasts) are unique paintings. They were done in 1405 for the old Cathedral of the Annunciation (built in 1397) by the three greatest painters of Ancient Rus: Feofan Grek, Andrei Rublyov and Prokhor of Gorodets. In the first, "local", tier of the iconostasis are icons dating to the 14th, 15th, 16th and 17th centuries. The prophets in the fourth tier are the work of mid-16th-century Pskov artists. The bronze moulding on the framework of the iconostasis and the half-length images of the patriarchs in the upper row date from the 19th century.

54. MURALS ON THE SOUTH WALL OF THE BEMA OF THE CATHEDRAL OF THE ANNUNCIATION. Painted in 1508 by Feodosy, son of Dionysius.

The subjects are: The Descent into Hell; the Eucharist-Communion in Wine (Communion in Bread is on the opposite wall); image of a holy man; the Washing of Feet; the Death of Ananias and Sapphira; and Christ's Apparition to the Apostles and Mary Magdalene after his Resurrection.

With his paintings Feodosy skilfully emphasises the walls, arches and vaults as separate parts of a single logical whole. The size of all his compositions and the number of figures strictly accords with the place of each in the interior. The compositions are made distinct not only by the lines that frame them but also by the 12 inward-facing countenances. The murals are a combination of fresco and tempera.

55—57. MOTHER OF GOD, JOHN THE BAPTIST and JOHN CHRYSOSTOM. The second tier of the iconostasis in the Cathedral of the Annunciation was painted by Feofan Grek in 1405.

Feofan gives his saints a very distinct personality: the Mother of God is a young woman of great beauty and majesty; John the Baptist is the withered hermit; and John Chrysostom, the fiery preacher. The images are executed in the broad manner of the monumentalist. Some information about Feofan's life is contained in a letter written around 1415 by the author Epifany the Wise to Kirill of Tver. Feofan was born in Constantinople, went to work in Rus and stayed there for 30 years.

In addition to his icons in the Cathedral of the Annunciation, there is a mural done by him in 1378 in the Church of Our Lord on Ilyin Street in Novgorod.

Wood, canvas, gesso, tempera.

Size of icons: Mother of God: 209 × 109 cm; John the Baptist: 210 × 109 cm; John Chrysostom: 210 × 103 cm.

Uncovered from later superimpositions in 1919.

58–59. THE APOSTLE PETER, an icon from the second tier of the iconostasis in the Cathedral of the Annunciation. Painted in 1405, possibly by Prokhor of Gorodets.

This image of the Apostle Peter, although quite in the style of Feofan Grek, is different in some respects. For one thing, Peter appears to be kindlier, his facial features are smaller and softer, and there is understanding and forgiveness in his look. The folds of his vestment are executed in the purely Russian manner.

There is no information at all about the artist himself, apart from a remark in the Chronicle that together with Feofan Grek and Andrei Rublyov he decorated the Cathedral of the Annunciation in the Moscow Kremlin in 1405.

Wood, canvas, gesso, tempera. Size 209 × 107 cm.

Uncovered from later superimpositions in 1919.

60–61. THE TRANSFIGURATION. THE LAST SUPPER. Icons from the "festive" tier of the iconostasis in the Cathedral of the Annunciation. Done in 1405, the former by Andrei Rublyov, and the latter by Prokhor of Gorodets.

Rublyov's images are sublime and lyrical. His compositions are straightforward and give the impression of serenity. The figures are executed in softly curving flowing lines. His colouring is a harmony of light transluscent and cool tints which make the whole composition remarkably weightless.

About Rublyov himself only a few facts are known. He was born either in 1360 or 1370, and died in 1430. He was a monk of the Troitse-Sergiev Monastery near Moscow, and later of the Andronikov Monastery in Moscow. He is famed for his frescoes, icons and miniatures. His genius was acclaimed in his lifetime, and for centuries his works served as models for the artists of the Moscow school.

Wood, canvas, gesso, tempera.

Size of icons: *The Transfiguration:* 80 × 60 cm; *The Last Supper:* 81 × 61 cm.

Uncovered from later superimpositions in 1919.

62. JONAH AND THE WHALE. A mural dating from the 1560s, in the north end of the gallery of the Cathedral of the Annunciation. A painting executed by an unknown artist in virtually a genre style. It illustrates the biblical story of Jonah, who was cast into the sea off a ship, was swallowed by a whale and then safely cast up on dry land; there he was met by the inhabitants of Nineveh, who turned from their evil ways under the prophet's influence.

The original colouring of the mural has been changed by numerous retouchings.

Uncovered from later superimpositions in 1930.

63–65. THE CATHEDRAL OF THE ARCHANGEL was built as a tomb of the Moscow grand princes by the architect Aleviz Novy in 1505–1508. Classical orders and details were used on its front for the first time in Rus. Seen from the north (Plate 63), the five-cupola arrangement is noticeably asymmetrical, because the west end contains staircases leading to the loggia. On the west front the staircases are marked by an elegant porch (Plate 65). The central

cupola of the cathedral, originally like the other four, was remodelled in the 18th century.

66. METROPOLITAN'S CHAIR in the bema of the Cathedral of the Archangel, made of white stone with a Renaissance shell and acanthus ornamentation.

67. INTERIOR OF THE VESTRY OF THE CATHEDRAL OF THE ARCHANGEL WITH MURALS AND THE TOMBS OF TSAR IVAN THE TERRIBLE AND HIS SONS IVAN AND FYODOR.

The murals date mainly from the mid-17th century. A part of the original early 16th-century mural, depicting the rich man's feast from a cycle on the parable of the life and death of the just man and the sinner, was found only on its south wall.

Church Slavonic inscriptions on the white stone slabs of the tombs, giving dates and names of the entombed, were carved in 1636–1637. The bronze lids were installed in 1903.

68. INTERIOR OF THE CENTRAL PART OF THE CATHEDRAL OF THE ARCHANGEL WITH 1652–1666 MURALS, ICONOSTASIS AND THE TOMB OF PRINCE DMITRY.

The team of painters who decorated the Cathedral in the 17th century was led by Yakov Kazanets and Stepan Resanets, two iconographers marked with special favours by the tsar. Later, in the 1660s (the work was done at long intervals), they were joined by the royal iconographer Simon Ushakov, and his follower Evtikhy Zubov. The main subjects of the murals are The Acts of the Archangel Michael, The Creed, and portraits of the entombed Moscow princes and the princes of other lands which were integrated with Moscow Principality as a united Russian State in the 15th and the early 16th centuries.

The murals were uncovered from later superimpositions in 1954–1955.

The Tomb of Prince Dmitry (a son of Ivan the Terrible), who, according to legend, was killed in the town of Uglich by Tsar Boris Godunov's men, has a white stone canopy dating from 1630.

69. DETAIL FROM THE GRILLE OF PRINCE DMITRY'S TOMB. On three sides the tomb is surrounded by a fine grille, an outstanding specimen of Russian cast-bronze work of the 17th century.

70. PRINCE ANDREI BOGOLYUBSKY. Detail from a 1652–1666 mural on the south-east pillar of the Cathedral of the Archangel.

71. THE BIBLICAL HERO GIDEON PURSUING HIS ENEMIES WITH THE HELP OF THE ARCHANGEL MICHAEL. Detail from the cycle of The Acts of the Archangel Michael (1652–1666), a mural on the south wall of the Cathedral of the Archangel.

72. THE ARCHANGEL MICHAEL AND HIS ACTS. An icon of the first quarter of the 15th century by an artist of Andrei Rublyov's circle. The Archangel Michael, the Commander-in-Chief of the celestial host, with outspread wings and sword in hand, is the image of youthful grace and terrible power. The panels portraying the Archangel's acts and especially the battle scenes are highly dramatic.

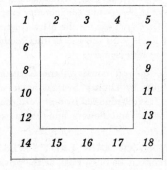

1	2	3	4	5
6				7
8				9
10				11
12				13
14	15	16	17	18

The subjects of the panels are as follows:
1. The Trinity. 2. In Council.

3. The Archangel smites the Assyrian troop with his sword. 4. The Archangel interprets the Prophet Daniel's vision of the beasts, personifying the kingdoms doomed to extinction: Babylonia, Macedonia, Persia, Rome and that of Antichrist. 5. The Archangel drives Satan away from the body of the Prophet Moses. 6. Jacob's Ladder. 7. The three youths in the fiery furnace. 8. The Archangel Michael's apparition to Joshua. 9. The Apostle Peter is led forth from the dungeon. 10. The apparition to Pakhomy of the Archangel Michael in the schema. 11. Jacob wrestles with the Archangel. 12. The destruction of the iniquitous city of Sodom. 13. The Archangel helps the hero Gideon to defeat the Midianites. 14. The Covenant. 15. King David orders Uriah into battle. 16. The Archangel drives King David from the bed of Bathsheba, Uriah's wife. 17. The Prophet Nathan rebukes King David. 18. The miracle in Colosse.

Wood, canvas, gesso, tempera. Size 235 × 182 cm.
In the "local" row of the iconostasis of the Cathedral of the Archangel.

73. JACOB WRESTLING WITH THE ARCHANGEL. A panel from the icon *The Archangel Michael and His Acts.*

74–76. IVAN THE GREAT BELFRY. A three-tier, slightly tapering campanile built in 1505–1508 by the architect Bon Fryazin. A superstructure was added to it in 1600 and a record of this was made in gold lettering on copper plates mounted in the cupola. The campanile with its cross towers to a height of 81 metres. It gave an excellent view of the territory around ancient Moscow over a radius of 30 kilometres. An intermural stone staircase leads up to the belfry and from there on ascent is by a metal ladder spiralling inside the cylindrical shaft.
To the north of the campanile stands a belfry built by the architect Petroche the Little in 1532–1543. To the north of the belfry a tower-like structure was added in 1624; it was named after Filaret, the Patriarch's church-warden. In 1812, the belfry and Filaret's wing were blown up by Napoleon's retreating troops, but the campanile escaped. The two former buildings were restored in 1816–1819 by Gilardi. Tsar Bell stands on a pedestal at the foot of the campanile.

77. TSAR BELL, seen from above. It was cast in the Kremlin by the Russian master Ivan Motorin and his son Mikhail in 1733–1735. During the great Moscow Fire of 1737, the bell, still in the moulding pit, but freed from its sand mould, became so hot that it cracked and a piece fell away. It lay in the earth in that state until 1836, when under Montferrand it was dug up and placed on a pedestal as an example of artistic casting. Weight: 200 tons; diameter: 5.85 metres; height: 6.14 metres.

78–81. THE CATHEDRAL OF THE TWELVE APOSTLES AND THE PATRIARCH'S CHAMBERS are a part of the once rambling Patriarchal Palace, which gradually fell into disuse after Peter the Great abolished the patriarchate in Russia in 1700 and instituted the Synod, a collegiate organ of Church administration. Restoration work on the Patriarch's Chambers and the Cathedral of the Twelve Apostles was started in the 1920s.
Construction work on the Patriarchal Palace began in 1643 under the direction of the stone-mason David Okhlebinin, and was continued under the famous Moscow architect, Antipa Konstantinov. In 1652–1656, the palace was largely rebuilt, with the Cathedral of the Twelve Apostles (Plate 78) and the great Hall of Crosses, used as an audience chamber and now known as the Chrism Chamber (Plate 80), newly erected.
On the north side of the palace there is still to be seen an arcade (Plates 79 and 81), a part of the gallery which joined the Patriarchal Palace to other buildings of the Kremlin.

82. A NIGHT VIEW OF THE KREMLIN'S SOBORNAYA SQUARE

III PALACES

83–87. GRANOVITAYA PALATA (Faceted Hall—Plate 84) was erected in 1487–1491 by Pietro Antonio Solario and Marco Ruffo, as a state-room for the palace built by Tsar Ivan III at the end of the 15th century. It was used for the reception of foreign envoys, councils of state and ceremonies to mark national holidays. It derives its name from its front of faceted blocks. In 1682 it was decorated by Simon Ushakov, but none of the murals has come down to us. At the same time, the windows were enlarged and embellished with Moscow Baroque platbands done in white stone by Osip Startsev (Plate 85). In the 19th century, the hall was redecorated by two Palekh painters, the Beloussov brothers. Of the original interior decoration there now remain only the carved gilt portals in white stone (Plate 87). With a total area of 495 sq. metres (Plate 86) the Faceted Hall was one of the biggest in 15th-century Russia.

88–89. THE TSARINA'S GOLDEN CHAMBER (Plate 89), situated over the 15th-century palace built by Ivan III, was erected in the second half of the 16th century for the Tsarina Irina (the wife of Fyodor, son of Ivan the Terrible), as a reception and banqueting hall. Carved gilt portals in white stone are still extant (Plate 88). The frescoes on the walls and the vaulting date to the late 19th century. Work carried out in 1947 shows that the original 16th-century frescoes are intact under the later layer. In the late 17th century, metal braces and a powerful arch were made to reinforce the vaulting when a chapel was erected on top of it.

90–93. TEREMNOY (BELVEDERE) PALACE was built in 1635–1636 by Ogurtsov, Konstantinov, Sharutin and Ushakov. It stands on two storeys of a 15th century royal palace. The façades of the fourth and fifth storeys are the most decorative (Plate 90). The so-called "petition window" (Plate 91)—petitions to the tsar were placed in a box lowered into the yard from the window—was much larger than the others and had a heavier platband.
The Golden Porch (Plate 92) led to the living quarters of the Teremnoy Palace. Its rich decorations are typical of Russian 17th-century architecture; this applies especially to the double hanging arches linked with carved heads of fantastic beasts in white stone (Plate 93). The portal was painted in the middle of the 19th century but fragments of the 17th-century originals were uncovered in 1949.

94–95. VERKHOSPASSKAYA PLATFORM, linking the Teremnoy Palace and the Verkhospassky Cathedral, dates from the second half of the 17th century. It is separated from the Golden Porch by the "Golden Grille", an excellent piece of gold-plated ironwork.

96–97. CORRIDOR AND STAIRCASE LEADING TO THE VERKHNY TEREMOK OF THE TEREMNOY PALACE. The elaborately carved archivolts and columns harmonising with the style of the whole palace were painted in the mid-19th century.

98–100. VERKHNY TEREMOK (Upper Belvedere) is situated on the fourth floor of the Teremnoy Palace. The entrance to it from an open walk is through a carved portal above which is a plaque setting forth the names of the architects and date of the building (Plate 98). The vaulting of the spacious well-lit chamber is covered with carvings. The murals date from the mid-19th century.

101. DETAIL OF A TILED STOVE IN THE THRONE CHAMBER

102. ANTECHAMBER IN THE TEREMNOY PALACE. A small chamber in which the boyars awaited the tsar's appearance. The white stone portals are covered with carvings, the floors are of wooden planks, and the stoves are encased in variegated coloured tiles. The frescoes on the walls and on the inner surfaces of the vaults date from the mid-19th century.

103. THRONE ROOM OF THE TEREMNOY PALACE, a royal reception chamber. The door on the left opens on to a staircase leading to the Verkhny Teremok; the door to the right admits to the pantry. The stove is a 19th-century imitation of an 18th-century stove. The wall paintings date from the mid-19th century.

104. BEDCHAMBER IN THE TEREMNOY PALACE. The bed and the murals date from the mid-19th century.

105. THE VERKHOSPASSKY CATHEDRAL, a royal family chapel, built by Bazhen Ogurtsov in 1637. The carved wood iconostasis dates from the first half of the 18th century. The icons on it

are from an earlier iconostasis and were painted by Zubov, Stepanov and Kostromitin, image painters of the late 17th century. The classical-style central part of the iconostasis of oxidised silver was fashioned in the second half of the 18th century.

106. LONGINUS THE CENTURION. The royal school of image painters of the 1680s, possibly the work of the royal iconographer Tikhon Filatyev of the Armoury.

The penitent Longinus is a lifelike portrait of the model. Tikhon Filatyev used a chiaroscuro technique to model the face and hands; his figures are on the bulky side, with artificial postures and gestures in the iconographic tradition.

Wood, canvas, gesso, tempera. Size 120 × 80 cm.

In the iconostasis of *Our Lord Behind the Golden Grille* in the Teremnoy Palace.

107–108. ICONOSTASIS with gilt high-relief carving fashioned in the early 18th century by wood carvers of the Armoury, for the Low Sunday Church of the Teremnoy Palace.

The framework of Russian iconostases from the 15th century to the first half of the 17th century was made of beams on which the icons were stood. These beams were covered with ornaments or low relief carvings. From the second half of the 17th century, elaborate gilt carvings (Plate 108) predominate over painted ornaments. Depending on the architectural and decorative design of such iconostases, icon frames could be round, octagonal, or other shapes.

109. POTESHNY (AMUSEMENT) PALACE was built in 1652 by the boyar Miloslavsky (father-in-law of Tsar Alexei Mikhailovich). In 1679, it became the tsar's property and was used for all manner of amusements. It was rebuilt several times, but in architectural character remained akin to the Teremnoy Palace.

110. CUPOLAS OF THE TEREMNOY CHAPELS, standing on brick drums which are overlaid with ceramic ornaments by the "monk Ippolit" (1670s).

IV PUBLIC BUILDINGS AND MONUMENTS

111. VIEW OF THE KREMLIN PALACES

112. TSAR CANNON testifies to the skill of Russian foundrymen. It was made by Andrei Chokhov in 1586. Weight 40 tons, calibre 89 cm. The cast-iron gun-carriage and the cannon-balls were made in the 1840s. No original cannon-balls remain.

113. THE ARSENAL. Construction work was started by Ivanov and Konrad in 1702 by order of Peter the Great. Work was interrupted from 1706 to 1722 by the Swedish war, and was finished in 1736 by Schumacher. In 1812, the building was blown up by the retreating French and restored in 1816–1826 by Bovet and Sokolov. More than 800 cannon, coming from every country in Europe and captured by the Russians from the French in 1812, line the front of the Arsenal. Unique 16th and 17th-century cannon are also on display here.

114–116. THE BUILDING NOW HOUSING THE COUNCIL OF MINISTERS OF THE U.S.S.R. was erected by Kazakov in 1776–1788. The main front faces the Arsenal with which it constitutes a symmetrical ensemble of the classical order, with a prominent central section. Of the inner premises, the best known is the Sverd-lovsky Hall, used as the meeting place of government bodies, for the presentation of awards, etc. An imposing Corinthian colonnade carries a drum surmounted with a lofty dome almost 25 metres across. The walls are covered with reliefs allegorising Education, Law, Jurisprudence, etc. The hall is 29 metres high.

The state flag of the Russian Soviet Federative Socialist Republic was raised here in March 1918. In 1922, it was replaced by the flag of the Union of Soviet Socialist Republics. The flat which Lenin occupied from 1918 to 1922 is in this building.

117–118. THE GRAND KREMLIN PALACE was built in 1838–1849 by Ton (*see* Frontispiece to Section IV) on the site of an ancient palace which had been repeatedly remodelled and had fallen into great disrepair by the mid-19th century. The state-rooms of the palace are decorated with the symbols and attributes of old Russian military orders. The Georgievsky Hall (Plate 117), commemorating the military order of St. George, is the most impressive. On its walls, faced with marble slabs, are carved the names of military units, generals and officers—among them Suvorov, Kutuzov and Ushakov—who had won this decoration between its inauguration and 1870. The marble statues on the entablatures of the pillars symbolise the Russian Army's major victories.

More than 20 rare woods were used in the elaborate parquetry design which is related to the various sections of the ceiling and the chandeliers. The hall is 61 metres long, 20 metres wide, and about 18 metres high.

It is now used for government receptions, as a lobby during the sessions of the Supreme Soviet of the U.S.S.R. and the Russian Federation, and other government and public meetings, and also for youth dances and New Year fir-tree parties.

In 1934 a noble hall was made by joining two state-rooms. It is the palace's largest hall, seating 3,000, where the Supreme Soviet of the U.S.S.R. now meets (Plate 118). Decorated in the neoclassical style, it was equipped with air conditioning, wired for radio relays in several languages, and with special lighting arrangements, etc.

It was remodelled by the architect Ivanov-Schietz. The statue of V. I. Lenin is by Merkurov.

119. THE KREMLIN THEATRE building was erected in 1930–1932 by Rehrberg, initially for administrative purposes; in 1958, its club was remodelled into a theatre by a team of architects and engineers led respectively by Pchelnikov and Segal, and Kondratyev and Fyodorov.

120–123. THE KREMLIN PALACE OF CONGRESSES was built in 1960–1961 for congresses, mass meetings, opera, ballet, and concerts. It was designed by a big team of architects under Posokhin, and a group of engineers under Lvov. It has an auditorium seating 6,000 and a banqueting hall for 2,500. The fifteen mosaic emblems of the Soviet Socialist Republics in the lobby (Plate 121) were designed by A. Deineka.

The walls of the auditorium are lined with imitation leather and a lattice work of golden ash and aluminium wire gauze (Plate 122). It has the most recent technical fitments, including acoustic electronic equipment, and earphones at each seat, relaying the speeches in 29 languages. The walls of the vestibules and the lobby are faced with stone and marble slabs brought from Siberia, the Urals, Georgia, and Armenia. The floors are connected by escalators.

From the banqueting hall there is access to a roof garden which gives an excellent view of the Kremlin's venerable pile, and a good deal of Moscow itself. Karel Neubert has caught the fairylike effect of the ancient Kremlin temples reflected in the palace's modern plate-glass windows (Plate 123).

124. VIEW OF THE NEW PART OF THE KREMLIN WITH THE MOSKVA RIVER

I WALLS AND TOWERS

1. Beklemishevskaya Tower. 1487
2. View of the Kremlin and the Moskva River
3. Spasskaya Tower. 1491
4. Red Square. The Lenin Mausoleum. 1929—1930
5. Spasskaya Tower
6. Nikolskaya Tower. 1492
7. Arsenal Tower. 1492
8. Kutafia (16th century) and Troitskaya Towers
9. Troitskaya Tower. 1495
10. Borovitskaya Tower. 1494
11. View of the Kremlin from beyond the Moskva River
12. South Wall and Towers along the Moskva River. 1485
13. Tainitskaya Tower. 1485
14. Beklemishevskaya Tower. 1487
15. Beklemishevskaya Tower.
16. Tsarskaya Tower. 1680
17. South-east Wall and Towers
18. Red Square from the Moskva River
19. St. Basil's Cathedral. 1555–1560
20. Vodovzvodnaya Tower. 1489

II ANCIENT PAINTINGS
AND ARCHITECTURE

21. Cupolas of the Teremnoy Chapels
22. Portal of the Church of the Nativity of Our Lady. 1393
23. Interior of the Church of the Nativity of Our Lady
24. The Cathedral of the Assumption. 1474–1479
25. Cupolas of the Cathedral of the Assumption
26. Iconostasis and Murals in the Cathedral of the Assumption
27. Inside View of the Vaulting in the Cathedral of the Assumption
28. Detail from a Mural in the Bema of the Cathedral of the Assumption. 1642–1643
29. *Adoration of the Magi.* Fresco in the Cathedral of the Assumption. 1480s
30. *Mother of God.* Detail from a Fresco in the Cathedral of the Assumption. 1480s
31. *St. George the Victorious.* Icon in the Cathedral of the Assumption. 12th century
32. *Our Lord of the Golden Hair.* Icon in the Cathedral of the Assumption. 13th century
33. *Apparition of the Archangel Michael to Joshua.* Icon in the Cathedral of the Assumption. Early 13th century
34. *The Chastening Eye of The Lord.* Icon in the Cathedral of the Assumption. 1340s
35. Angel. Detail from the Icon, *Old Testament Trinity,* in the Cathedral of the Assumption. First half of the 14th century
36. The Apostle Paul. Detail from the Icon, *The Apostles Peter and Paul,* in the Cathedral of the Assumption. Late 14th century
37. *Our Lady of Vladimir.* Icon in the Cathedral of the Assumption. Early 15th century
38. *In Thee Rejoice.* Icon in the Cathedral of the Assumption. 1480s
39. *The Apocalypse.* Detail from an Icon in the Cathedral of the Assumption. Late 15th – early 16th century
40. *Metropolitan Pyotr and His Life.* Icon in the

124